MYSTERIOUS STORIES FOR INTELLIGENT MINDS

By Justin Copson

Respective authors own all copyrights not held by the publisher.

The information herein is offered for informational purposes solely, and is universal as so. The presentation of the information is without contract or any type of guarantee assurance.

The trademarks that are used are without any consent, and the publication of the trademark is without permission or backing by the trademark owner. All trademarks and brands within this book are for clarifying purposes only and are the owned by the owners themselves, not affiliated with this document.

Table of Contents

Before you start reading, scan this QR Code to get all bonus content!

INTRODUCTION

Life is filled with many surprises. There are more things we didn't know about life than things we know about life. At every point in our lives, we get reminded of existing things, but we never get to see and experience them.

Have you ever thought about thinking about something you never thought about, talking about something you never talked about, finding out things you never found out, and experiencing things you never knew happened? Well, this book is the only one in the world to offer you that opportunity.

It's worth noting that all information in this book is confirmed, irrespective of how impossible some of them look. They happened somewhere, sometime.

Everyone has their history to make. Accessing the information in this book will show you how you didn't need much effort to make your history.

What history are you making?

CHAPTER 1: FASCINATING CULTURE YOU NEVER KNEW EXISTED

AUSTRALIA

Australia is known for many beautiful things. You can't talk about the beautiful things in Australia without talking about culture. You might never find several cultures in Australia or any other part of the world. One of these cultures is the cockroach race. Yes, you heard it right - cockroach race.

Have you ever imagined what happens before an Olympic tournament? Just think carefully before giving your answer. The fact will always remain that whoever will represent their country in the Olympics will always be very good at what they do. You can't be going to race in the Olympic tournament when you're sluggish at running. Once you're on the race, all eyes are on you. Even as you run as fast as you can, the eyes of the whole world are on you. While some would wish you became tired or slower or even got out of the race, others from your country wish you could be faster and win. This must be how a race works. Imagine when it becomes a cockroach representing humans in the Olympic race.

Some people might see it as weird, but it's a culture in Australia valued by so many people. The most exciting thing about the cockroach race in Australia is that the whole of the 26th of January is picked out as a special day for the race.

During Thanksgiving in the United States, family members travel from different parts of the country for a family reunion. You get to see people you haven't seen in a long while and have fun with them. Enjoy a good dinner with them and talk about many things that happened while you were apart. Americans always look forward to Thanksgiving. Although celebrated in other parts of the world, it's a culture that is too important to Americans. Imagine looking forward to a cockroach race and having family members gather on the 26th of January to watch the cockroach race. Family members in Australia could travel over a long distance in Australia to meet other family members so they could watch cockroach races.

By the 27th of January, when kids sit in their classroom or at any place they find themselves together, what will they be talking about? Of course, it has to be a cockroach race. They must tell their friends how they enjoyed their cockroach race day. They'll like to boast about how their uncle, whom they haven't seen for many months, came around and bought gifts or how their mom took them to a nice place to watch the cockroach race. And, when the teacher would be teaching in the class, you could still hear them whisper about the cockroach race day.

The kids are not the only ones allowed to talk about the cockroach race. How could they be the only ones talking about it when adults are the ones who get more involved in the cockroach race? By the 27th of January, adults have a lot to share about how they spent their cockroach race day.

You'll have to see many people talking about it at their workplace. This could bring a lot of smiles and laughter to those talking about it.

One peculiar thing about the cockroach race that has made it endure for a long time in Australia, even to this day, is that it can make one rich or broke in a single day. Imagine walking up to a place, spending about thirty minutes there, and then walking out as a millionaire. Do you think that's always possible? Well, it's possible with the cockroach race, and this is how: while many people get involved in the cockroach race for fun, some involve themselves actively in it to make a lot of cash. What these people do is that they stake a bet on which cockroach will win a race, and if this cockroach wins the race, they walk home with a lot of money. So, while the cockroach could be very sluggish in its race and might not be close to being as fast as the lady or guy representing their country in the Olympic race, a lot of people still watch it with a lot of anxiety since they know a win would land them a lot of money that would eventually change their lives for good.

But everyone doesn't walk home smiling after a cockroach race. For someone to win in a tournament, another person has to lose. It's not just about race, and it's the same in almost every aspect of life. Think about it: for one to be referred to as the best student in a class, there should at least be a lot of other students they're better than. During an election, for one to win, there should be others that will have to lose the election. Likewise, for someone to walk home smiling after winning a bet placed on a cockroach race, another person has to walk home fighting to lose a bet placed on a cockroach race.

While the cockroach race might not be common in other parts of the world, it means a lot to many Australians. That's what culture is all about. It could look strange but meaningful and fascinating to others who see it as their culture. (947)

JAPAN

We can't talk about countries with the most weird culture without mentioning Japan. Japan is known for many festivals that mean a lot to the locals around there, but this one never makes sense to people who are not from Japan - Naki Sumo Misturi.

One beautiful thing about vacationing in another country is that you get exposed to cultures and traditions that are so different from the ones you've come to get used to. You get to see stuff you've never seen before, and this stuff you see becomes part of the beautiful memories you'll never forget. You'll get to talk about it even ten years after leaving the country. The quest for building beautiful memories is always why people visit different sites and places on vacation. It's also the reason a lot of people prefer to visit a country during a particular festival or a particular cultural celebration. But what will you make out of Naki Sumo Misturi if you visit Japan when it's being celebrated? This question will be left to answer after finding out what Naki Sumo Misturi is all about.

Naki Sumo Misturi is a festival about watching a crying baby. We don't mean a doll or a robot resembling a baby. When we say a baby, we mean a real baby, and this baby will have to be crying.

When you see a baby crying, what comes to mind? It means the baby is uncomfortable about something or asking for a change in something they didn't like. If an adult finds himself in a situation he's uncomfortable with, he tries to walk away from it. This is because he has functional legs, legs that can walk him out of that place that puts him in a lot of discomfort. Of course, there are situations that adults will find themselves in, and they might not be able to walk away from those situations even though they feel very uncomfortable in them. When this happens, the adult will still have to complain about it. They'll have to be vocal about it.

They'll talk to the person they believe has the solution to that very uncomfortable situation they struggle with. If they can't find someone with the solution to the problem, they'll at least talk to other people around them, hoping that one of them will at least have a solution or know someone with a solution to the problem they find themselves in. What about when the adult can't walk away from the uncomfortable situation and can't talk about it? There are non-verbal ways the adult can still make it known that they're uncomfortable with it. It could show on their face.

They could just be frowning, and just from looking at their face, someone will find out they're not happy with the situation they had found themselves in. But in the case of babies, they can't walk away from their problems. They've legs that are too young to stand firmly on the ground and walk away from situations they find themselves in.

They've mouths that should have at least been used to talk about the exact thing they're uncomfortable about, but there's no way they would be talking about it since they don't even know how to make a speech. The only thing they could use to tell those around them that they're very uncomfortable with what is happening to them or what is happening around them is crying.

Once they start crying, people around them get notified that they're uncomfortable with something happening to them or around them, and these people start trying to see if they can change the situation. This is why if a mom is cooking in the kitchen and hears the baby crying in the livingroom, they try to go quickly to the livingroom to find out what is happening. Nobody enjoys leaving a baby to cry, but the Naki Sumo Misturi festival is all about this.

During Naki Sumo Misturi, the baby will have to cry to the delight of people. Instead of stopping this baby from crying, the adults around will watch in delight. The baby's cry is a very important period for this festival. It's the most crucial moment. Many people pay attention to getting the exact details of the result by themselves because, among other babies involved in this festival, only one baby has to come out as the winner. For this baby to emerge as the winner, careful attention is needed. This is why being attentive matters in this festival.

What it takes for a baby to win is crying louder than other babies. For a baby to emerge as a winner from the Naki Sumo Misturi festival, the baby has to be the one with the most heard cry among other crying babies. So, while moms in other countries would always find a problem with their kids crying a lot, it could mean something important to a mom in Japan. A mom in the United States could be worried about her baby crying loudly all the time, while a mom in Japan could be happy and save it for the tournament.

What if, during the Naki Sumo Misturi festival, the baby that has to participate in the crying competition refuses to cry? This is an important question that would be in the minds of many creative minds. Babies are always known to disappoint us when we never expect them to. Most times, the behavior of a baby could be very predictable. A mom already knows some of the predictable behaviors of her baby. She already knows how her baby will react to a particular situation, which could be different from how another baby would react. But this still doesn't change the fact that babies could, at one point, be unpredictable.

When you want them to laugh, they might refuse to laugh, no matter what you do to make them laugh, and when you don't expect them to cry, they could continue crying, leaving you confused about why they're crying. So, there are possibilities that when a baby is brought to be part of the festival, the baby might refuse to cry, which could end up ruining everything.

Do they beat the baby that refuses to cry so that the baby will cry? No, they don't beat them, but they still make them cry. It would look inhuman for a lot of people for a parent to beat a baby so that they would cry to the delight of a festival. Of course, it would also seem inhuman to the Japanese, so they don't beat the baby to make the baby cry. They use a mask to get the job done.

If you're familiar with babies, you'll know they get scared when they see something that looks scary. Once they're scared, they'll have to cry. Without beating the babies, the adults must wear a very scary mask. They'll then have to carry the baby and make the baby look at them. It's natural for babies to try to look at the faces of those carrying them. But if they're not looking, the adults will still make them look. Once they look at the faces of the adults putting on the very scary masks, they're bound to be very scared. They'll start crying.

This is when the judges will try to find out which baby cries louder than other babies. The one that cries louder than the rest eventually becomes the winner. The baby's mom will end up being so proud of her baby for winning the festival, even without knowing what is happening around them. (1440)

CHINA

One common tradition in most Asian countries that has lasted for centuries is the chopsticks. We can't ever separate most Asian countries from their chopsticks. Of course, they use spoons at one point, but chopsticks will always remain special.

When we talk about Asian countries, which country first comes to mind? It has to be China. China has always been one of the ten most popular countries globally. China is popular for many things, especially the chopsticks. You can't visit China and not at least eat with chopsticks. It's a culture that has endured for hundreds of years. This is understandable considering the kind of dishes that are predominant in China. While it might look uncomfortable for an outsider watching Chinese eating with chopsticks on a TV, visiting China will make you realize how difficult it is to eat some Chinese dishes with a normal spoon. At one point, you'll find yourself borrowing some help from the chopstick.

As simple as the chopsticks might appear, this tradition of chopsticks in China is never spoken of but is observed by almost everybody. It's the tradition of not keeping the chopstick upright in a rice bowl.

When we talk about culture and traditions, we find many people observing certain cultures and traditions without even knowing why they're observing them. The majority of people also grow up observing a certain culture they never knew a thing about. They just grew up finding themselves living that way. They might have gotten used to seeing their parents and other people around them living that way, so they grew up living that way. One thing about kids is that they try to learn from what they find others around them doing. It doesn't matter whether the person they're learning from is an adult or a kid. This is why environmental issues are essential in the life of a child. The child is very much attached to their environment and always tries to live according to what their environment portrays. The child is like a representative of their environment. If their environment is bad, the child will most likely misbehave, but if their environment is good, the child will have to act in a good way that represents their environment.

Why do you go about putting on shoes? It's because you grew up seeing people around you putting on shoes. Why do you go about putting on clothes? It's because you grew up seeing people putting on clothes. Why do Chinese and many other Asian citizens eat with chopsticks? It's because they grew up seeing people around them eating with chopsticks. We can bet that a Chinese that grows in an American home in America where they don't use chopsticks will not know how to use them.

But why don't the Chinese keep their chopsticks upright in a rice bowl? It has a lot to do with a tradition for the dead. The Chinese have a lot of respect for their dead. Not just the Chinese but also most other Asian countries. Most Asian countries have rituals for their deads, and whenever they do, they always make sure they've food and drinks, which they believe their dead would also eat. In China, food is also offered to the dead, and rice is believed to mean a lot to the deceased. As a result of a particular ritual meant for the dead, the Chinese don't keep their chopsticks at an upright level in their rice bowl. What a way to respect the dead. (630)

ETHIOPIA

Have you been to East Africa before? When we talk about East Africa, what country comes to mind? Kenya? Recently, Kenya has seemed to be the most popular country in East Africa because of its fast-growing economy, but we can't talk about East Africa without talking about Ethiopia. Ethiopia is one of the oldest known African countries with a very relevant history presence.

When we talk about beauty, what do you think? What comes to mind? Beauty means a lot of things to a lot of people. But, in general terms, when something is beautiful, it should be something that can be recognised at first glance. Humans will generally say that a woman is beautiful just from looking at her face and body appearance. We can also say that a man is handsome just from looking at his face and other body features. Of course, other unseen features can contribute to one's beauty, but we're not considering those we can't see. We're interested in those that are before our eyes.

We've always heard people say "beauty is in the eyes of the beholder," of course, this is also true because someone that a person believes is beautiful could also be said not to be attractive by another person. This is where love comes in. Love has a way of making someone who might not be beautiful to one person to be beautiful to another person. But we aren't talking about love. We're talking about beauty.

Do you know the current most beautiful lady in the world? What's her name? Yes, that's what beauty is. She became the most beautiful lady in the world because she's gorgeous. At least, just from looking at her, almost everybody will agree that she's beautiful.

What about the most handsome man in the world? Almost everyone would agree that the most beautiful man in the world is attractive. Everyone doesn't need to agree, but at least many people should.

That's the kind of beauty we're talking about, a beauty that is recognized by many to be beautiful. A beauty that when you come to the United States and say that it's beautiful, someone in China would agree with the fact that the beauty is sure beautiful. When it is decided that it's beautiful in Russia, many people in the UK will agree that it's true.

But, the Bodi tribe in Ethiopia have a way of measuring what true beauty means to them, and it's not the same way the rest of the world sees it.

In the United States, obesity is becoming something a lot of people are working so hard to avoid. Nobody wants to find themselves in a situation where they would be diagnosed with obesity. There are a lot of health concerns concerning obesity. Health experts will tell you that you're at a high risk of suffering from a handful of diseases if you happen to become obese.

In the United States, many people believe beauty has much to do with one's weight. While there are people who wouldn't mind how big a man or a woman appears, there are a lot of people who would prefer to go out with someone who isn't fat. It's not just in the United States; it's the same in most parts of the world, and we'll prove that to you.

The thing about your favorite movie heroes is. Those movie heroes you grew up loving, those you tried mimicking as a child. Think about those movie heroes you fell in love with as you grew up. What do they look like to you? Of course, movie heroes come in big sizes, but most have slim appearances or appearances that wouldn't be said to be fat. Once you're watching an action movie, you get to see that most of the heroes in those movies are not overweight. Those beautiful girls in movies that make you want to fall in love or those handsome boys in your favorite movies that make you wish you could grow quickly and meet your Mr Right, they mostly don't appear fat. This is because the world can make beauty look perfect, even though this might not always be true.

The Bodi tribe in Ethiopia are not shy of telling the world what they think true beauty is all about. To them, a handsome man is that man with a bigger look. If you want to be seen a a hero, you've to appear big, and it doesn't matter whether it's natural or not.

As a result of the believe of this tribe in Ethiopia, a lot of people feel depressed when they find out they've a slim figure. These people wish they were born to look somewhat obese.

In the United States today, a lot of people are working tirelessly to lose some of their weight. Some go for surgery, some stick to the gym, some watch their diet, and stick to a very disciplined lifestyle so as to make sure they don't become obese. The reverse is the case in the Bodi tribe. While a lot of people in different parts of the world are working morning and night to lose weight, people in the Bodi tribe are working tirelessly to gain weight.

Gaining weight is so serious to the Bodi men that they've to live their homes and go on a self-inflicted exile. They don't want anything that will distract them from gaining weight. So, they believe separating themselves from people around them will make them focus on gaining weight. They dedicate a period of six months to gaining weight. During this period of six months, every one of their activities is channeled towards how to become fat. During this period of six months, one very common food they feed on is a mixture of milk and blood. They consume a large percentage of milk and blood on a daily basis for six months until they believe they're fat enough to present themselves to the public.

During the new year, the fat men present themselves as a form of contest. During this ceremony, the fattest man is crowned the hero. He's seen as the most handsome man in the tribe. He retains this honor throughout his lifetime. Winning this contest means a lot to every man from the Bodi tribe. It's just like winning a gold medal in the Olympic tournament. Who wouldn't like to be the most handsome in their society? (1112)

CHAPTER 2: PARANORMAL REALITIES YOU WILL NEVER BELIEVE HAPPENED

THE LOST VILLAGE

The story of the lost village is a story that was told by a woman about her experience in Scotland. The story was first published in 1942. The story revealed something that not just everyone would have seen on every normal day.

The woman in this story was having a walk with her husband. They were both having some conversation as they walked beside each other through an ancient forest. Then, they decided to take a shortcut through the Wild Glen. They were intending to walk down the bank of the Fillen to Crianlarich. Before this time, they never had any strange thing off from normal in mind because they were just having the normal conversation every husband and wife would have while walking beside each other.

There's this thing about people being very observant about their surroundings. You can have a couple of people walk down a street together, and just one person will get to notice something that every other person wouldn't notice. Why? Because this one person was observant. Some things might just happen within a second, and no one might get to notice them unless there's someone who is very observant, someone who has a strong connection with their surroundings to see things before they get by. This was exactly what happened while this woman and her husband were walking on this shortcut they decided to take.

In this case, her husband seemed to be sensing something about the surroundings, which his wife had yet to start noticing: "I don't like this place. It's too old and dead," he said to his wife. He wasn't seeing anything; he wasn't hoping to see anything, but he was feeling something strong from the surroundings. While he said this to his wife, his wife was thinking something that was quite different from what her husband was saying he was feeling about the place. According to her, she believed the place was a peaceful place since it was quiet and didn't seem to have much disturbance from people. People rarely walked through this place, and there was hardly any activity going on around here. She was going to explain to her husband how peaceful the place was, but her body suddenly started feeling something she would never forget for the rest of her life.

Before that moment, she had only felt peace from her surroundings, but what she started feeling was a strong sensation of depression and hopelessness. She didn't know why she was feeling this way. This made her not continue with what she was going to say to her husband. She told herself that something wasn't right. Of course, she had been to a lot of peaceful places, places where she would like to go whenever she wanted to clear her mind of things that were bothering her, places where she would like to go to so as to get some touch of nature. She had initially thought she was feeling the same peaceful aura she had felt in those places, but the sudden change surprised her.

Perhaps this woman wouldn't have been able to explain why she suddenly started feeling the way she felt if the whole thing had ended with what she suddenly started feeling. It didn't end there. According to her, just when she was still having depressing feelings and hopelessness from the surroundings enveloping her, she saw herself feeling as if she was in a snow, under a leaden sky, and behind her were people with their eyes looking hopeless. She was frightened. She knew that there were really no people there other than her and her husband, and there was no reasonable explanation for what she had just witnessed. Her husband then looked at her, and he could see how frightened she had turned into. They had to leave there as quickly as they could towards their destination.

She told her husband about what she had experienced. It further confirmed what he had felt about the place. They got to the hotel where they were headed, and they couldn't keep what they had felt to themselves. They told people there about what they had experienced. According to the woman, when they talked to people about what they experienced, Mr

Alistair Stewart said to them, "Oh yes, that would be where a whole village was lost in the snow, and they all starved to death."

According to the woman, even if she was chased by Hiler and his grizzly gang, she would never enter that forest again.

THE HORSE WHISPERER

The story of the horse Whisperer was told by a woman who owned an old farm that was initially owned by a family called Hawkins. The Hawkins used to live on the farm. At least three generations of the Hawkins family lived on this farm before this woman came to the farm. The story was first published in 1970, as it was told by B. Whynell-Mayow, who claimed the woman who owned the farm told him the story.

So, this woman suddenly acquired the property and was the new owner. She never suspected anything when she started working on the farm. She had her children, who were helping her out on the farm. They never suspected anything strange about the farm. Of course, if they did, they never would have moved into the property.

After working on the farm for a while, there was something they started noticing about the farm that they didn't have any explanation for. According to what the new owner said, she said there were times she would be at home with her kids, and they would be perceiving the smell of tobacco. It felt completely strange to her and her children. At first, they thought that there were people smoking tobacco somewhere on the farm or maybe from the farm surroundings. If this was true, it should have at least not been frequent.

Like, maybe someone would have been passing through there and might be smoking tobacco as they passed through or maybe someone decided to stay around the surrounding bush and have a smoke. Yes, these would have seemed reasonable. But the thing that didn't add up was the fact that the smell of tobacco didn't cease. There were times when the smell would be perceived during nighttime or during odd hours, and no one would have been at those spots; they might have suspected that someone might be staying and smoking.

One thing about certain truths is that they might be too strong for us to accept. Some truths might look too unreasonable to accept, but it doesn't change the fact that they're the truth. For this woman, while she and her children were trying to find out where the smell of tobacco was coming from, she had this thought within her that the smell wasn't coming from the farm surroundings. The smell was coming from within.

The most tricky thing about the situation of this woman who was living on the farm with her children was the fact that she had never smoked tobacco in her life, and none of her children were smoking tobacco. None of them were smoking tobacco, but they kept perceiving the smell of tobacco from within. It only meant that there was something beyond the ordinary that was happening. But it didn't stop at just perceiving the smell of tobacco; there was something more that surprised this woman about this new farm that she had acquired.

She owned a young female horse, which she loved so much at the time. This horse meant a lot to her, and she would sometimes hang around with it. The farm was big and mostly lonely. It was a life she enjoyed, and having horse company made it fun. So this horse got pregnant at one point, and this woman cared for it until around when the horse was due for delivery. The horse had difficulty in delivering its young. It had a complication that made it to be in pain. This woman was distressed by the situation.

Animals can't talk like humans, but they're like babies. When babies are bothered about something, they cry to get the attention of their parents. It's the same with animals. Once they find themselves in a difficult situation, they let out their cry in their own ways. Sometimes, we might not be able to change the course of nature, but we can at least do certain things to help them get by the difficult situation they find themselves in, and that was what this woman decided to do.

She wanted to help her horse by consoling it in the difficult situation it found itself in. She was also very distressed because she was scared that something would happen to her horse, who was also a good friend to her.

The woman went to the stable to help her mare. Immediately she walked into the stable, she felt a presence that wasn't just that of her horse. She also noticed that despite the pains the horse was going through, the horse felt somewhat comforted, but there was more. She also started perceiving old Hawkins' smoke. The smell was in the stable this time, but she couldn't see anyone who was smoking in the stable. This further made her realize that despite the fact she was living on the property with her kids, they weren't really alone on the property.

The incident with her mare made her become very curious about the things she had noticed since she moved into the farm with her children. She hadn't really asked questions before then, but the incident with the horse got her attention. It was obvious that someone was comforting her horse.

Whoever that was doing that must have been the same person or group of people that were smoking the tobacco. Whomever it was was kind to her horse, so she believed the person or people had good hearts.

The new owner of the farm had to ask people whom she believed could tell her things that would help her find out stuff she never knew about the farm. She believed there was a story behind what she had experienced. So, she had this gardener who knew a lot about the farm. He was, in fact, one of the Hawkinses and was brought up on the farm before the new owner came and acquired the property. After she acquired the property, she still decided to work for her. She talked to this gardener about the stuff she had observed. It was after she had talked to him that he told her that all the family were devoted to animals and that they all smoked pipes. The revelation made a lot of sense to the new owner.

THE GHOST RESTAURANT IN NIGERIA

Have you ever heard about a restaurant run by a ghost? The last time we actually heard about something like this was in a South Korean series titled "Hotel del Luna." It wasn't really a restaurant. In the movie, there was this hotel where ghosts could book and stay around for a while before they would transition to the next place. Most of the ghosts that stayed in this hotel were mainly ghosts who believed they had some unfinished business to take care of before they died. So, while staying in this hotel, they would try as much as they could to settle this business so that by the time they would eventually be leaving and transitioning to the next place, they wouldn't have to leave in regret.

But the story that happened in Nigeria sometime in 2022 wasn't a movie. It happened somewhere in Lagos, one of the most busiest cities in Nigeria. So, there was this restaurant that a lot of people in the neighborhood always visited to have their meals. The food that was served in this restaurant was known to be the best. They taste exceptionally. According to those who had gone to the restaurant to have their meals, they had particularly talked a lot about the amala dish served in the restaurant.

Amala is a dish that is peculiar to the Yoruba tribe. It is known to be the main traditional dish of the Yoruba tribe. The main ingredient used in making amala is yam. There are some Yoruba soups which blend well with amala. For one to eat amala, one would have to eat with one of those soups.

So, this restaurant already made the record for itself as the best when it came to serving amala dishes.

When you have a restaurant that serves very good dishes that would make you come back for more, one peculiar thing that should be noticed about such restaurants is the fact that they would most likely cost more than other restaurants. Like, if you want to have your favorite dish in such a restaurant, it should at least cost more than others in the same neighborhood. But the odd thing about this restaurant was that the meals weren't expensive. You would have a wonderful meal at a very low price. This made a lot of people always prefer to go to this restaurant for their meals.

A lot of people who were going to their work in the morning would stop by the restaurant to have their breakfast. There were some who would stop by for their lunch during work hours. The customers were huge and overwhelming.

The staff at this restaurant were said to be one of the best. They were kind and made sure they rendered the best services. This made it almost impossible for one to have any reason to complain about this restaurant. There were a lot of people recommending the restaurant to their friends, and whenever their friends went to this restaurant, they always came back with good stories about the food and the pattern of services rendered. Everything was just too perfect to be true, and that's what the problem was.

History has continued to tell us that when something is just too perfect to be true, then it might not be true. When we look at history and the stories about the experiences people had found themselves in, we'll get to see thousands of stories about how things that were too good to be true turned out to become something that people had feard and dreaded the most. The disappointment that comes from stuff like this becomes so glaring that those who experience it never get to forget it for a very long time in their lives.

So, there was this particular person that came into the neighborhood where the restaurant was located in Lagos. Someone recommended the small restaurant to him. The person had told him a lot of good stuff about the restaurant and how he would always prefer to return there to have his meals after having his first meal there. The person that was recommended became curious because of the so many things that were said to him about the restaurant. He decided to go experience things by himself.

When he got to the restaurant, he waited for one of the staff to come attend to him. There were about four of them in total that were running the restaurant. By the time one of them came around to attend to him, he was shocked beyond measure. He felt goosebumps all over his body. It felt like he was dreaming. He had to ask himself again and again if what he was seeing was really a reality. It happened that the person who was coming to attend to him was someone he knew from the past.

She wasn't just someone he knew from the past, she was someone he would never forget. The big twist wasn't just that he knew her from the past. If the problem was that he had known her from the past, he wouldn't have felt that much shocked and had goosebumps all over his body. The most they could do was to be happy to meet each other after so many years of being apart and then maybe get each other's phone numbers if they still wanted to continue communicating. But, this would never have been possible in this case since the situation was a very abnormal one. The lady he had just seen walking up to him to find out what he would want to eat from the menu of the restaurant was someone he knew to be dead in the past.

He knew when she died, how she died, and attended her burial. He didn't think there was any way he would ever find her again, at least not in this life. But, what he was seeing was beyond human comprehension. According to him, he had heard stories about how people die and go to a distant place to live another life. This normally happens when the person who has died fails to achieve certain things that were so important to him, which he wanted to achieve, and which no one would have possibly helped him achieve after he had died. As a result of the strong desire to achieve this very thing, the person stays back, but in another place where he might never be recognized by anyone. He lived most of his life there. Most times, these people finally get recognized by someone who knew them from the past. Even though this man had heard a lot of stories like this, he never got to witness it by himself.

The lady was approaching him, but she had yet to recognize him, even though he had already recognized her. On getting before him, she asked him what he would like to be served. It was at this point that he managed to call her by her name, which everyone who knew her used to call her in the past. Immediately, he called her by the name, and she vanished from existence. It was just like a movie scene that this man couldn't believe it. He was so shocked that he couldn't speak a word. Everything seemed to have happened too fast to him.

After he had collected himself, he was expecting that another staff would at least approach him to say something, but none of them did. He wasn't even feeling like having his meal there again. He was too scared to even think of having a meal there. After he collected himself, he was curious about the woman that had vanished. He wanted to know more about how she had been living and how she had managed to go about living her life even though she was really dead. He needed to know what staying around her was like and if those around her didn't notice anything weird about her throughout the times they had shared with her without knowing she was a ghost.

The only people he could really talk to were the staff that were working with her at the restaurant. He believed that there was no way the staff wouldn't have at least a few things to say about her. He had told himself that after listening to the stories of the staff, he would then inform them about the fact that she was dead. This was because he felt it wasn't fair for a dead person to be making and serving people's meals.

So, this man stayed in the restaurant for a moment, but no other staff approached him to say anything to him. He decided to go meet them by himself. He had initially seen them having some conversations earlier. On getting to where he had found them earlier, none of the staff was present. It felt odd to him. He looked around, but within the restaurant, there was no staff member that he could find. He was thrown into deep confusion. He had questions that he needed answers to, and he couldn't find those he had wanted to ask those questions to. At first, he couldn't make anything out of it until he found out that they had abandoned most of what they were doing and had vanished when the first woman he had identified vanished. The fact that he found out was that all of the staff working in the restaurant were actually dead at different times in the past. Identifying one of them felt like identifying all of them, and this was why they had to vanish. It was at this point that this man let out a loud scream that caught people's attention.

A lot of people came around to know what was happening in the restaurant, and this man narrated what had happened to them. The people were thrown into panic. This was because they had all had meals in the restaurant at different times in the past without suspecting anything. The thought of eating a meal that was prepared by a ghost felt like they were going to die at any moment. The story just couldn't make any sense to a lot of people because there was just no sense in a group of ghosts coming together to open a restaurant. They must have sat together and planned the whole thing together.

The news about the restaurant spread like wildfire. A lot of people came around to see things for themselves, and they found it the way they were told. Most of them remained scared because they had felt that something bad might happen to them because they had at one point had their meals in the restaurant.

THE GHOST FRIEND

The story of the ghost friend was told by one of the friends who happened to be alive after her best friend died. These ladies were very good friends who did a lot of things together. They shared a lot of secrets together as they told each other things they never would have said to any other person. The friendship was so strong because of how sincere they were with each other.

Sincerity builds a very strong bond. Most friendships these days have failed to build strong bonds between those involved in them because either one or both of those involved in these friendships are not sincere to their friends. With the way the world has turned, it continues to become difficult to find people who practice true sincerity. Everyone is looking for something to gain from someone else. Even married people who are bound in love hardly live with sincerity among each other. This is why we've a lot of people moving their separate ways. People are just after what they would gain for themselves, and they would do everything against those around them so as to achieve their objectives.

Lack of sincerity is the main reason we have a lot of selfish people out there. Selfishness makes it difficult or even impossible for a lot of people to be trusted. No one would like to trust someone who would turn around tomorrow and betray them. The world has turned into a place where everyone is being too careful of those around them. The meaningfulness of life had continued to be degraded to the point that life had continued to be more meaningless than meaningful. That's what lack of sincerity had led the world into. But we still have people who practice sincerity, and every once in a while, they have this experience that no one would ever have. The same happened to one of these friends.

So, while these ladies were going about being good friends with each other, a lot of things were happening in their respective lives. They had their families living in different parts of the country. One day, one of the girls received a call from her parents. They wanted her to come home because they had something they wanted to discuss with her. This lady was living in a different state from her parent and was attending school. Her parents kept asking her to come around, and they probably missed her. She agreed she would be going to see them in the state where they were staying. She had siblings in the state where she was attending school. This kind of made her mostly take a while before she would be traveling to see her parents. But this time around, her parents wanted to see her.

On the day the lady would be going to see her parents, she was going to meet her best friend, but she couldn't. She left without meeting her even though she had promised she was going to meet her and spend the night at her place and then travel to see her parent from her place. Things didn't work out that way. So, she traveled.

A day after she travelled, she returned back and went straight to her friend's home. Her friend was quite surprised to see her. She never expected she would be returning that soon, but she was happy to see her. They spent a lot of time together discussing a lot of fun things. They laughed at each other's jokes more than they used to in the past. Then, it was time to make dinner. The friend that had just returned from the travel decided she would be the one to make dinner. She made noodles for them to eat for dinner. The night was a long night for them. Whenever they stayed together at night, they talked a lot, but that night was different. They talked more than they used to. Her friend, who had just returned from her travel, told her a lot of things about herself which she had yet to tell her. Even while the other friend was sleepy, she continued talking until she eventually slept off.

The next morning, the two friends spent a brief time together since they both had places they had to go that morning. The one that had just returned from her travel left first.

Later, at noon, the friend who was visited at her place by the friend who returned from travel and was walking around a busy place to get something for herself heard someone calling her. The voice felt familiar, so she looked to see who it was. It was the older brother of her friend, who she had spent the night with. The older brother had a sad look on his face. She couldn't understand why he was looking at her, and she could guess he had been crying. Before she could say anything to him, he told her that her friend was dead.

The lady was shocked. She couldn't process what he had said immediately. She had thoughts about the both of them being together throughout the previous night and how they were both together during the morning. It was just some hours ago that they separated. It didn't make sense to her. She could see that the young man was not joking. There was no way he would approach her and tell her that her friend was dead when her friend was not dead. It was a joke that no one would like to get themselves involved in. It took the lady a while to compose herself. She still believed that something was not right. She then tried to inquire when her friend died.

The older brother told her that her friend had travelled to see their parents, but she never saw their parents again. She got involved in an accident on the road and died before she could get to see their parents. It felt like a lie to this lady. It felt like the whole story was cooked up. It took her a while to agree to the story. What the story meant was that her friend who had come to stay with her at her home after she had returned from her travel was a ghost.

Her friend actually died on her way to see her parents. She had wanted to spend some time with her before travelling, but she couldn't. She felt so bad about this and had her friend on her mind even while she traveled. After she got involved in the accident that took her life, she still felt bothered about promising her friend that she was going to come spend time with her and not showing up as promised. She decided to go spend time with her friend even after she had died.

It was a very heartbreaking experience for this friend. Everything now started adding up. She told her a lot of things about herself that she had yet to tell her. This was because she knew she was a sincere friend. One thing her friend regretted the most was falling asleep while she was still talking. At first, after she was told that her friend was dead, and after she realized that she had stayed with a ghost the previous day and during the early hours of the morning, she was scared, particularly because the ghost of her friend cooked dinner which they ate together. But, months after of the incident happened, she wished she had spent more time with her friend. She wished she hadn't slept while her friend was conversing with her. She had a lot of regrets. If she knew it was the last time she would be spending with her friend, there was a lot of stuff she should have done with her and a lot of things she should have said to her. But she felt special because her friend saw how sincere she was. She saw how pure her heart was, and that was why she came back to spend a last moment with her even after she was dead.

Time, they say, is the most expensive thing that can never be bought. If people could buy time, a lot of billionaires would still be alive today. Life doesn't stay forever. Time continues to tick, and it never returns. When we meet good people, it matters a lot to be good to them. It matters a lot to be sincere with them. It's only when we're sincere to those around us that we'll be able to share strong bonds that will help us build beautiful memories with them. Life is flitting; after time had passed, some people would die. When these people die, what will remain alive will be the beautiful memories we build with them. It matters a lot to be a good person to people around us.

CHAPTER 3: STRANGE THINGS ABOUT SCIENCE SCIENCE

THE UNLUCKY DOG OWNER

Do you've got a dog? If you do have a dog, what does your dog mean to you?

To many, their dogs are their pets that should never be separated from them, no matter what. No matter how bad things go with them, they want their dog to always remain beside them. To some other people, their dogs are not pets to them, and their dogs are family. There are limits to privileges given to a pet, but to a family, there are obviously more privileges.

Dogs are no doubt man's best friends. Their love for humans knows no bounds. A dog can do anything to protect its human friend, even if it involves laying down its life to protect human its human friend. Stuff like this had happened again and again. So, the love of a dog has never been questionable.

Some years ago, there was a man in Wisconsin named Greg Manteufei. He had this dog he loved so much. They shared a strong bond with each other. Just like every other dog owner, he had always believed his dog would never do anything to intentionally harm him. He had heard of stories about how accidents happen, and people get hurt by their own dogs, and he believed that there was no way a dog would hurt its owner. Most of the time, a dog hurts its owner; it is always as a result of a misunderstanding or wrong interpretation of the situation at hand by the dog. A dog might harm its owner while trying to protect him. There are a lot of things a dog could see that the owner might not be seeing, and while trying to protect its owner from those things, the owner might end up getting hurt in the process.

Some dog species have been recorded to have issues with interpreting situations at some points; these species end up hurting their owners without having the intention to do that. Incidents like this have happened several times with these dog species. This is why a lot of people have been advised not to keep those species of dogs that could turn around and attack them after misinterpreting something.

Greg's situation was different. His dog never attacked him or did anything to cause him injuries. His problem came from his dog showing him too much love. Think about it: have you ever seen a situation where people find themselves at a strong disadvantage because of the love shown to them? Have you seen people find themselves in difficult situations after those who care about them show them how much they care about them?

Well, there's this popular saying about life that things should be done in moderation. Nothing is good when they're done in excess. Love is a beautiful thing, but when love becomes too much too extreme, it becomes a problem. In humans, when love becomes too extreme, it can push one into doing things that they never should have done. For example, someone could love his girlfriend to the point of using his tuition fees to buy her a birthday gift. Well, that's love, but it's a problem because it has led someone to do extreme things they shouldn't do. Another example is when people love people to the extreme to the point that they would do bad things to make them happy.

A love that would make one go to extreme levels to make the other person happy is not good, especially when it would make you do bad things to make the other person happy. Some people might go out there and steal so as to make the other person happy; that's not how love should be. Some people will hurt their parents so as to make the other person happy; that's also not how love should be. Love should make you always want to do good things, not bad things.

But too much love will make you want to do things without thinking, so it becomes a problem. Apart from love, what about other areas of life? Studying your book is good, but when you study at every hour of the day and do not make time for other things, it becomes a problem. No matter how much you want to study, you should at least make out time for other things that will bring a lot of fun into your life. Playing is good. Everybody, including adults, needs a little play for life to look lively, but when one plays too much, it becomes a problem.

A student who plays too much and does not make out time to study his books will most likely end up having a bad grade. Alcohol is good for adults who want to take them. It's not compulsory to take alcohol. In fact, life is better without alcohol, but for adults who want to take them, there are no problems at all, but when they get taken in large quantities, it becomes a problem. Too much alcohol might become poison to the body and could cause more damage than one could ever imagine. Watching movies is interesting, but have you ever tried watching movies from morning till night none stop? When you try watching a movie from morning till night, the movie might end up losing its sweetness, and you might end up having a headache because you watched a lot of movies.

Nothing is good when they're done in excess. It's the same for the love of a dog. This became clearer in the case of Greg and his dog. When a dog loves you, they always want to be around you. They'll always want to cease whatever opportunity they've to lick you. You become their everything to them, and that was what happened in Greg's situation. His dog loves him so much and wants to always be around him. One thing his dog enjoys is lick Greg. Greg found out that his dog enjoyed licking him; it was one of its ways of showing Greg how much it loved him. Humans would kiss people they love. For dogs, they would also want to kiss, but they do their own through licking.

So, at every given time, Greg's dog would lick him. He never found anything wrong with this, and no one said there was anything wrong with this. But Greg's dog loved him too much, so he was always licking Greg more than he should, and Greg never complained. He just left his dog to do whatever it liked. This happened for some years; it became a norm for Greg's dog to lick Greg several times in a single day.

So, at one point in Greg's life, Greg started noticing things he didn't understand how to give an explanation to them. His body was feeling strange to him. Of course, Greg had been sick severally in the past, and he had

gotten himself treated in the hospital during those times that he became sick. There were sicknesses that had affected him severely in the past. Like, these sicknesses happened repeatedly. So, whenever Greg was sick, he could guess that one of those sicknesses was what he was suffering from. But what he was feeling at this point was something he had never felt before. It felt completely strange as if his body was beginning not to be his body. When it started, it wasn't that serious, so he didn't complain much about it.

It affected his hand and leg. He had thought they were one of those normal things that would happen to someone, and they would disappear on their own, but it didn't happen in this case. At one point, Greg decided to take what was happening to him seriously. It's not like he never took it seriously, just that what was happening to him came up too quickly before he could visit the hospital. So, when he visited the hospital, the doctor diagnosed him. What was happening to him was beyond normal. They had to check again and again to be sure about what they were suspecting. The result for the diagnosis came out the same after they had checked several.

They had to check several because what they had found out wasn't something that was common in humans. From the result, Greg was infected by a particular bacteria called Capnocytophaga. This bacteria lives in most household pests, including dogs. It happened that Greg's dog had this bacteria. One very surprising thing about this bacteria was that when it happens to be in these household pests, it doesn't cause any harm to them. But once they're passed across to humans through bites or scratches and then find their way into the person's bloodstream, they can result in deadly problems. Dr Silva Munoz-Price, an infectious disease specialist, told Live Science that what was happening to Greg was rare. There was very little possibility of someone finding himself or herself in the situation that

Greg found himself in. It almost will not happen, but since it happened to Greg, there are still possibilities that it will happen.

Greg had thought that after he had been diagnosed, he would just go through some treatment, and everything would just be okay, but the case was more serious than he had thought. Of course, this had happened to a lot of people. They might find themselves struggling with a particular disease which they believed wasn't too serious, but by the time they get diagnosed and start going through treatment, they get to find out that the disease they had looked down on has the capacity to change their lives forever.

When we talk about life changes, life changes are easier when you expect them, when you see them coming. When you expect a life change, you gradually plan yourself towards it. You make provisions that would help you walk through those life changes. You put a lot of plans in place and do a lot of things in anticipation of those life changes. By the time those life changes will come, you'll find out that they won't bother you as they would have bothered you if you didn't plan for them. This is because you already had a lot of measures put in place that would help you overcome them. But when these changes come suddenly without you being prepared for them, without you making plans for them, they change your life completely. You'll most likely go through a lot of misery while trying to adapt to the sudden changes that find their way into your life. Some people might end up giving up after failing to adapt to the sudden changes that came into their lives. This is because they didn't plan for it; they didn't see it coming. If they had planned for it, they would have at least put a lot of things in place that would help them adapt better to those changes as they come.

In Greg's case, the change that came with his diagnosis was sudden, and it hit on him so hard that he had to make a very quick decision to save his life. The doctor had to be truthful with him, and the truth was that he would have to amputate his legs and arms to stay alive.

Greg saw his life change within a short period of time without him planning for it. He wasn't giving the time to think much about the situation he found himself in. He amputated his legs and arms and started adjusting his life to the new change he found himself in.

THE FART DISCOVERY

One thing that a lot of people never enjoy falling victim to is being somewhere and having someone farting in your presence. When people fart, in most cases, it is followed by a smell that no one enjoys perceiving, not even the person that had released the fart.

As uncommon as this might sound, the truth is that everyone does fart from time to time; just that the realities we see around us make it look as if this is not really happening.

Do you've got a phone? Look up the picture of the president of the United States of America. The president of America is one of the most powerful figures in the world. There's hardly any country where the president of the United States is not known. When the president of the United States says something, other World leaders listen. It doesn't matter whether what the president of the United States says makes sense or not; what matters is that the president of the United States is talking. The office commands respect. But, despite the respect the office of the president of the United States commands, the president still farts, and sometimes, he could do it secretly during a conference, and no one would find out. While looking at the picture of the president, you might be tempted to think that there's no way this man would fart, but he does really fart.

Who is your favorite celebrity? Perhaps he or she appears very spotless in public. When they're in public, they've got this thing about them that makes them look so perfect, and sometimes you'll wonder if they're even humans because of how beautiful or handsome they're. They make you wish you could ever have the kind of life they're having, and they make you wish you could live just like them. But the truth is that they fart. They do let out some farts, and the fart does smell bad.

So, irrespective of whomever one was or whatever status one occupies, they do fart, just as you do fart. Why? Because they're humans just as you're humans.

Researchers have been doing experiments on farts so they could make mindblowing discoveries about farts, and after years of scientific experiments, findings revealed something about farts which you can never imagine.

Do you know that just by farting, you could be releasing some amount of energy that could be used in creating an atomic bomb? According to scientific findings, if you fart consistently for six years and nine months, you would be releasing enough gas that will be used to produce the quantity of energy that will be used in creating an atomic bomb. What this means is that a lot of people have already released quantities of energy that are enough to create several atomic bombs just from farting regularly. So, next time you go about wasting your fart, think about how best to conserve it an use it in creating inventions that will change the world.

DOGS DETECTION OF EARTH'S MAGNETIC FIELD

Dogs are exceptional creatures that can serve a lot of purposes for different people, depending on what their needs are.

When an elderly person is always alone and complaining about loneliness, a dog becomes what comes to mind. A dog will always be there and will keep more than just company. Most elderly people have overcome depression and loneliness as a result of having a dog at home.

Loneliness is not only peculiar among elderly people. There are a lot of young people that need company. These people happen to find themselves in a situation where they're battling loneliness, and dogs become the answer to their problem. At the same time, they found it difficult to have humans around them that would keep them company; dogs filled the space and brought a lot of liveliness into their lives.

Some people are not lonely, and they just need to share their love with others. These people probably have a lot of love to give, but there's no one they could share this love with. Dog solves the problem. They find love in the dog, and they return as much love to their dog.

Some people need someone to protect them, but they've no one to protect them. Dog solves the problem. Dog protects them and makes sure there's no harm coming to them.

Security has always been a very important part of human existence. Humans have always had a high regard for security. This is because for every other aspect of human living to move smoothly, there's a need for proper security. Think about it: for businesses to move smoothly, there should at least be security. For people to go to their stores and sell their groceries and other important stuff, they've to be sure they're secured. For people to go to these stores to buy stuff, they've to be sure they are secured. For people to invest in real estate in a particular place, they've to be sure the place is secured. For people to carry out any sports activity at any place, they've to be sure their lives are secured. So, security has a lot to do with everything man does. Now, the police use dogs to deliver security services, and dogs perform really just fine.

Dogs already occupied a very important sport in human lives, and now scientists have discovered something about dogs and the earth's magnetic fields. What were they really thinking? Life, how did they come about stuff like this? There is no best way to arrive at a reasonable answer; all we know is that scientists have something to say about dogs and Earth's magnetic field, and it's a very interesting discovery.

One very funny something about this discovery that was made about dogs is that this discovery has to do with dog poop. Yes, you heard it right, dog poop. The discovery was first made in 2013 after an extensive scientific research.

Do you have a dog? It's common to see people who have dogs these days, but if you don't have one, there will hardly be any way you wouldn't know someone who has one. At least once in a while, you should have observed dogs popping. A scientific discovery found out that when dogs poop, they just don't start pooping towards any direction; they mostly align themselves to face the North or South pole of the earth. Now, don't you think this is weird? Even some humans don't know the direction of the North and South poles of the earth, but a dog would always make sure it is facing the North or South poles of the earth whenever it wants to poop. This goes a long way to show that dogs are actually more organized than they're being given credit for.

When we talk about pooping while facing the North or South Pole, no dog is exempted from this trait, both young and old. They always make sure they're facing either of the two poles of the earth's magnetic field. Now, if you're having a problem with detecting the direction of the earth's North and South poles of the earth's magnetic field, perhaps you'll have to wait until when your dog starts popping.

After making surprising findings about the most preferred directions dogs prefer to face whenever they want to poop, scientists decided to make findings about the direction they face whenever they want to urinate. They found certain differences in the directions dogs prefer to face whenever they want to pass out urine. In the research on the most preferred directions dogs face while urinating, scientists found out that female dogs also face the North or South pole of the earth's magnetic field whenever they want to urinate. However, the findings with the male dogs varied at this point. Male dogs would also urinate while facing the North or South pole of the earth's magnetic field, but it wasn't something they did all the time. Male dogs didn't mind urinating while facing any direction they preferred, and they had no particular direction they preferred to face.

After the scientific study, it was concluded that dogs prefer to face the North or South pole of the earth's magnetic field whenever they're poopping because they're sensitive to the earth's magnetic field. In other words, they've strong connections with the earth's magnetic field. One would not cease to wonder about the kind of connection a dog that doesn't know anything about science would have with the earth's magnetic field.

DEATH IS CAUSED BY TOO MUCH WATER.

Sometime in August 2023, there was this news that took the world by surprise, and a lot of people found themselves becoming scared of the bottles of water at their homes. Imagine doctors telling someone that they shouldn't drink water, that they would die if they drank a lot of water. It would be a difficult thing to accept, but it became something that Ashley Summers struggled with. In her own situation, no one warned her about the danger she might find herself in if she happened to drink a lot of water, and eventually, things went out of hand.

Between food and water, which do you think is more important? A lot of people will be too quick to choose food to be more important than water. But, have you ever found yourself in a situation where you're feeling tasty and very restless about it as if you're going to have serious problems if you don't drink water in the next few minutes?

Water has been said to be one of the most important liquids required for normal living. The body will have a lot of difficulty in functioning properly without water. In fact, the body isn't going to function without water. Water is needed for the body to digest food. Water is needed for the transportation of materials in the body. Water is needed for the production of saliva and other important hormones in the body. Think about most of the activities happening inside the body; most of them require water to get things working. Also, taking enough water has always been linked to healthy living. The skin, for example, needs enough water to glow. Different scientific findings have proved that people who drink enough water have healthier skin than those who don't consume enough water.

Water helps flush harmful substances out of the body. This is why scientists believe that people who consume enough water will hardly become sick because most of those substances that would have made them to become sick might have been flushed out by water. Water is said to be very good for the kidney. Research has proved that taking enough water would be very helpful for the kidneys to function properly and stay away from getting sick. But

Ashley Summers died from consuming a lot of water, and a lot of people are yet to know why this happened, even though findings have shown why this happened to her.

She didn't die because she consumed too much water; she died because she consumed too much water "too quickly." The best way to explain this while using ten litres of water will be a comparison of two situations where someone drinks ten litres of water in a single day and when one drinks ten litres of water within four hours. Ten litres of water is big for one to drink in a single day, but when one drinks it in a single day, the person would be said to have consumed a lot of water, but when another person consumes this same quantity of water within two to four hours, we'll sat they consumed too much water "too quickly."

Ashley Summers was said to have died of water toxication. She kept drinking water and even had to tell her family that she couldn't drink enough water to satisfy her taste. She continued drinking until she eventually collapsed from drinking too much water. Her situation was a rare condition.

The question that will come to mind is, what is water toxification?

Water toxification is a situation that occurs when someone consumes too much amount of water within a short period of time. The water in the body is regulated by the kidneys. After some quantity of water that goes into the body has served the purpose of going into the body, the kidney excretes some of the water from the body, thereby maintaining some degree of balance in the body. Everything in the body is meant to function at a healthy balance. Of course, when there is a bit of a shift from the balance, different parts of the body are meant to help in regulating them.

The kidney takes charge of the water and makes sure that the water in the body is not too much and is not too small. The kidney has to function at its own pace and not be pressured in any way. Think about when someone is pressured to perform a particular task. When people are under pressure, they might even end up making mistakes on things they were very good at.

It happens to everyone, even people who are professionals in a particular field. The kidney is not exempted. When one takes too much water within a very short period of time at a very quick rate, the body has too much water than is required. The implication is that the kidney will have to perform its work of regulating the water in the body, but in this situation, the water is not just the normal quantity of water that the kidney has been used to.

The quantity of water is extremely too much. The kidney might have to perform five times more than it used to perform in the past. This will make the kidneys to become too exhausted. Once the kidney becomes exhausted, it starts failing to perform its functions the way it should have performed it. This could lead to the dilution of electrolytes, particularly sodium. In simpler terms, the sodium goes off balance. This was exactly what happened to Ashley Summers.

Symptoms of water toxication could include nausea, headache, cramps, seizures, brain swelling, and in extreme cases, like in Ashley's case, could lead to death.

This discovery, as a result of Ashley's death, showed how important it is for people to do things within a balanced range. As was said earlier, nothing done in excess yields good results.

CHAPTER 4: WEIRD INVENTIONS

MASS SHAVING MACHINE

One distinctive difference between humans and other animals is that humans are intelligent. Every animal is intelligent in their own way. Have you watched a wild life show on the TV or a movie that shows what happens in the wild? When you watch this movie, you'll see different levels of intelligence of different wild animals. The lion could sight a prey from a far place and would start moving towards the prey in a stylish way that would make the prey not to know that there is a lion around. This lion might continue walking towards this prey of it until it gets close enough to dive at it.

The level of intelligence shown by the lion that helps it capture this prey is high. Do you know a single lion can't actually win an elephant in a fight? But once a herd of lions are hungry, they could come together and put their intelligence together and then attack an elephant. They win most of the time. While in the wild, when a small prey notices that its life is at risk, it employs its high level of intelligence to escape.

While the wild animal chasing after it will be putting its intelligence on the line to capture the prey, the prey will be putting its intelligence on the line to escape and live for another day. What about birds? Birds are intelligent enough to build their nest by themselves. They already know that if they lay their eggs just in the air or on the tree, they could fall off to the ground. So, they're intelligent enough to build a nest for themselves. When you look at different animals and some of their ways of living, you'll see different levels of intelligence, but despite this intelligence, man was said to be an intelligent animal over all of these other lower animals; why? Because man is the father of all inventions.

At every point in a man's life, he's thinking about what to invent to solve a problem. This is why the world was able to change a lot from what it used to be in the past. Think about the modern homes built by man today. Today, we've pen houses that are so long as if they would touch the sky. When we look at cars, we get to see them in different forms and prices. When we look at clothes worn by men, we see a lot of different designs. The invention of man and the lower animals are on different levels. Man has always been far above other animals when it comes to making inventions; this is how they were able to think about making a mass shaving machine.

Shaving had always been something that had been associated with men, even though a lot of women shave, too. In the past, men had used very crude tools to shave their beards. There were different issues with most of these inventions, and each time, the man continued to work really hard to make an invention that would be better with no issues. With the intention of making a machine that will solve several shaving problems at the same time, the mass shaving machine was made.

What does a mass shaving machine really mean? Think carefully; you can really answer this by breaking the words and then putting them back together. Yes, you must have gotten it right.

A mass shaving machine is a machine that can shave several people at the same time. What this means is that this machine has the capacity to shave like five different people at the same time. Think about the possibility of the current technological advancement. Do you think it's possible for five people to be shaved at the same time by a single person? Well, it doesn't look like something that is reasonable. This is because there's no way a single person can be looking at the faces of five different people at the same time.

Humans have two eyes, but there's no way the two eyes can focus on different faces at the same time. Once one of the eyes was looking at a spot, the other eye followed without being invited. That's how the human eyes work, but how was it possible to invent a mass-shaving machine? How did they make use of this mass-shaving machine?

The mass shaving machine was first invented in the 19th century. The machine was so incredible that a single barber could use it to shave a dozen men at the same time. Don't you think it sounds strange? With the human eyes always focussing on a single place at the same time, how can a barber really shave a dozen men at the same time? The truth is that while the barber's attention would be focused on a single place, there are chances that the other person might get injured by one of the blades of the shaving machine.

We know shaving is one thing that requires a lot of care and attention. While shaving someone's beard, the barber will have to be careful so they don't end up getting them injured or making the whole process too uncomfortable for them. This is one good reason the barber's attention had to be fully focused on the person that is being shaved, but the mass shaving machine was shaving several people at the same time, making it impossible for a barber to focus on all of those that were being shaved at the same time.

Another big issue with this shaving machine was that this machine couldn't change the direction of its movement according to the shape of the face of an individual. If you've ever shaved your beards, or have ever shaved someone's beards or have watched when someone's beards were being shaved, you'll get to realize how important changing the direction of the shaving machine is during shaving.

You'll have to change the direction from time to time to have a good shave. And, you don't just change the direction without any thought in mind. Changing direction has to be according to the face of the person that is being shaved. People have different shapes and sizes of the face. When these people have been shaved, one would have to move the shaving machine according to the shape and size of the face of the person that is being shaved. The shaving machine had this issue. It couldn't move according to the shape and size of the face of all of those it was shaving at the same time. This became another big issue with this mass-shaving machine.

At one point, it became unreasonable to continue using this machine. If such a machine has to be used in the current day, there will be a lot of problems. Compare the beards of people today and the beards of most of the men in the 19th century, and you'll see a lot of difference. While most men these days might not want to shave their beards entirely, they still need to shave to make their beards look good without shaving everything. They maintain different styles of beards, something that wasn't too common in the 19th century. If the mass shaving machine had to be used to shave these men, there's no way it would be able to do the right job on these men. The implication will be that most of these men might go home, losing their beards. It never would end with a smile.

ANTI-EATING FACE MASK

The anti-eating face mask is another invention that will never cease to amuse someone.

A lot of people never knew they would find themselves putting on a mask until the world found itself struggling with the COVID-19 pandemic that shook the whole world at the same time. Imagine one disease tormenting every corner of the world at the same time. It was a scary experience that so many families are still struggling to recover from their nightmare.

When you look at history, masks have been won for several different reasons. There are parties that one would attend, and one would have to put on a mask to avoid being detected. While at this party, it's allowed for people to stay and do their things the way they wanted to get it done while having their masks on. One can also decide to put on a mask to conceal his identity as a result of the nature of his job. When you watch modern wrestling today, there are wrestlers who have been performing without their real faces known to the world. Once they're on the ring, they put on a mask to conceal their faces. Their fans cheer them without knowing what their real face looks like. Apart from wrestlers, there had been musicians in the past who had put on masks to conceal their identities. The problem with this is that these people could just go out on the streets, and no one would know who they are, but it's good for them in some ways because they'll have their private lives all to themselves.

Celebrities always have big issues with maintaining their private lives the way they want them. No matter how much they try to live their private lives, their job will always continue to bring people around them, and this could sometimes make life to start being boring to them because there would be no way they could go around to do what other normal people do. Other people who have, from time to time, had reasons to put on masks are people working in security units.

There are police officers who always prefer to put on masks whenever they're on official reasons. There are military personnel who prefer to put on masks whenever they're on a sensitive mission. There are very important reasons for this. By putting on masks, these people hide their identities, and they get to protect their lives and the lives of their loved ones. Reprisal attacks have always been one big problem that always affects most people working for security units. They could go out there to discharge their duties as permitted by the law. But, while discharging their duties, a criminal might decide to take an act of revenge on them.

This criminal, after seeing the faces of these security officers, might decide to target their family members. Another reason why people put on masks is to hide their crimes. It's no longer news that whenever robbers try to rob a bank, they make sure they're on masks so that no one will get to see their faces. By putting on a mask, they could walk out of the bank after carrying out their crime with no one tracing it back to them.

So, there are so many reasons why people go about putting on a mask, but eating has never been part of it until the anti-eating face mask was made.

Food is one of the most important necessities of life. Everyone needs food to survive. We need food for our body to continue carrying out its normal functions. But, over the years, it has been found out that there are people who love food more than others. And, when one loves food just too much, it could become a problem to them in certain ways. There are a lot of issues that could come up from loving food a lot or losing control when one sees food or certain types of food. In most cases, it could be something that has to do with one's health. The doctor might say, don't eat this, but once the person sees what the doctor had recommended they shouldn't eat, they start having a strong urge to eat it because this happens to be something they had enjoyed eating for several years.

Food addiction is a big problem that will be so difficult to solve. There are different forms of addiction, and there has never been an addiction that is easy to stop. A lot of people who are smoking cigarettes must have thought that once they wanted to stop smoking, it wouldn't be a difficult thing to do. So, they continued smoking for a long period of their lives until, at one point, they decided that they wanted to stop. At that point, when they decided they wanted to stop smoking, they realized how almost impossible it was for them to stop smoking.

They do everything they can to make themselves to stop smoking, but the more they do everything they can, the more the habit continues to persist.

It's not just smoking, and you can also see the same trait in those who abuse other substances like cocaine, for example. Cocaine is a very addictive substance. A lot of people started abusing cocaine, thinking that they were on top of their game and could stop at will, but after years of struggling with the addiction, they found out how difficult it is for one to quit abusing cocaine. One very big problem with abusing cocaine is that it has a way of turning one's life upside down.

A lot of people become very broke from abusing cocaine. It has a way of messing with one's brain and makes the person to lose focus in most of the things they do. Most cocaine addicts get fired from their jobs because of their inability to do their work properly at their places of work. Before these people got fired from their work, they must have been depending heavily on their jobs to fund their addiction.

But after they get fired from their job, they exhaust their savings to fund their addiction. After exhausting their savings, they start selling off their properties and also start taking debts to fund their addiction. A lot of life gets ruined by substance abuse. The effects they leave on those who abuse them are very bad. Some people became criminals over a crime they committed while they were high on a substance they abused.

These people wouldn't have committed those crimes if they were in their right state of mind, but they weren't in their right state of mind. They were high on a substance, and this led them to do things that eventually destroyed their lives.

When we compare substance/drug addiction and food addiction, which do you think would be easier to stop?

Most of those substances that are abused happen to be substances that don't add any value to the lives of those who abuse them. They tend to be substances that the body doesn't really need for anything. The body doesn't need alcohol to perform its normal function. The body doesn't need cigarettes to perform its normal function. Also, the body doesn't need cocaine to perform its normal function.

What about food? The body can't function without food. There have been articles released on those who try to starve themselves of food for some days. Some of them end up losing a lot of weight and becoming very sick. Some of them who are not lucky enough end up dying as a result of starving for too long. So, without eating, one could die. But without smoking, taking cocaine, and taking alcohol, one wouldn't die.

So, when one is addicted to abusing food, there is a big problem because it would be so difficult to stop. This is because you need to eat every day to survive. When there is too much food to eat, you'll have to eat until you're full and then stop. But in most cases, those who are addicted to abusing food don't get to stop when they're meant to stop, and it causes a lot of issues for them. Most times, these people happen to find themselves suffering from obesity. It was believed that anti-eating face masks could help to solve this issue.

There was this time when an anti-eating face mask was recommended for a chef and others working in a restaurant. There are people who can't stay around food without at least trying to put some of the food particles into their mouths. While there are a lot of chefs who wouldn't feel like eating while cooking, there are a handful of chefs who might end up eating most of what they're cooking while cooking them.

Take, for example, a chef baking something delicious or a chef frying meat. It could be tempting for some of them to eat some of the baked food or fried food. When a chef forms the habit of eating some of the stuff they cook while cooking them, it becomes a big problem for them because, by the time they are done cooking, they will have eaten a large quantity of the food they're meant to cook. This is one good reason the anti-food face mask was invented.

Staff in restaurants could also have issues with staying around food and holding themselves from eating them.

When one has different dishes of delicious food around them, and they can't hold themselves from eating them, and they've free access to eating them, what do you think will be stopping them from eating them? This was another reason for inventing the anti-eating face mask. Some restaurant owners believed that with the anti-eating face masks, they could reduce the loss they make from their staff eating large quantities of their food while on duty.

It'll surprise you to know that housewives were also among those for whom the anti-eating face mask was recommended. It was believed that there were housewives who had issues with keeping themselves from eating some of the foods they baked or some of the foods they fried. Some of these housewives end up eating large quantities of these foods before they would be able to be done in the kitchen. For most of them, it was a habit they built over a long period of time that they couldn't suppress once they were in the kitchen and cooking for their family. As a result of this, it was believed that the anti-eating face mask would help them handle this issue.

The question to ask is this: Does an anti-eating face mask really solve the problem of eating when one shouldn't be eating? Perhaps it might, but the issue with one eating when they shouldn't is more strongly about discipline. The truth is that even with having the anti-eating face mask on, some people could still take them off and eat whatever they wanted to eat, but it was still a good, innovative invention.

SUITCASE SCOOTER

Have you ever thought about using your suitcase for transportation? Whoever came up with the idea must have been a genius.

The first time this was spotted was believed to be in China in the street of Changsha.

All over the world, transportation has always been a big source of concern. Considering the fact that the cost of owning a car continues to go higher, people will have to work really hard to own their own car. Owning a car isn't an easy job since one would at least need to spend some money from time to time to maintain their car. The cost of maintaining a car isn't easy at all. What if one needs to maintain their car at a point where they're broke? But, recently, we've had more problems to deal with than just maintaining a car. The price of gas had continued to go higher. For one to buy gas for their car, they'll have to spend more than they used to spend in the past.

The implication is that it has an effect on the price of transportation. There are sectors of the economy that have a sharp effect on the prices of goods and services; one of them is the price of gas. When gas is more expensive than it ought to be, it'll cost more to transport goods and will most likely cost more to buy those goods after they have been transported.

As a result of the continuous rise in the price of transportation, a lot of people have continued to think about ways they could make things easier for themselves. Making things easier for themselves had always been a trait in humans that often made them stand out from other animals.

Humans generally love free things or things that would be gotten out of almost nothing. The problem with these free things is that they're not properly valued. Most of the human inventions that happen to be properly valued till these days happen to be things that were acquired at a high price.

The quest for cheap or free transportation led to the discovery of suicide scooters.

The suitcase scooter was first believed to be made by He Liang in China. He didn't want to continue spending most of his earnings on transportation, and he wanted something he could use to go home without spending much on it, something that would make his daily life so easy for him. This was why he embarked on his ten years of work of inventing his suicide scooter. He spent the ten years modifying the suitcase into a motor-driven vehicle that could carry him to wherever he wanted to go to. The suitcase was believed to have a top speed of 20 km/h and the power capacity to travel at 60 km.

One very interesting thing about this invention that was made by He Liang was that he was able to drive it around without the use of gas. He was trying to prevent himself from spending on transportation, and he believed it wouldn't make any sense for him to spend on this invention of his. He didn't want the price of gas to affect his daily living, and as a result of this, he constructed the suicide scooter in a way that it would have to be charged before it would be used. It lasted for a long before the charged power would run out.

An invention of this magnitude should have been mass-produced and distributed to every part of the world. But surprisingly, a lot of people never knew about this. This invention would make one move their luggage with ease. Think about it, and you could want to take a flight to travel to another country, you wouldn't need to go to the airport with your car or look for a taxi, all you've to do will be to get on your suitcase and drive to the airport with everything you need for your travel inside the same suitcase you're driving to the airport. Another advantage of the suitcase scooter, which is far ahead of most of the cars we've today, is that it operates without the use of gas. One wouldn't have to always spend money to get gas whenever they wanted to transport themselves to anywhere they intended to go. Then, the bigger advantage, which reflects to the current trend most world leaders are working so hard to achieve, is that this suitcase scooter wouldn't pollute the environment. It works with renewable energy. One wouldn't need to burn fuel and pollute the environment while making use of the suitcase scooter. What an interesting way to save the environment.

THE FLYING SAUCER

When you hear about a saucer, what comes to mind? Aliens, right?

We can't talk about saucers without talking about aliens, thanks to most of the modern twenty-first-century movies. Most of the movies made about aliens were particularly linked to aliens moving on a saucer. There were a lot of science-fiction movies that were made with aliens moving into the earth on a saucer to carry out an important mission. Although there had been a lot of movies these days about aliens that never had links to them flying on a saucer, but the early movies done on aliens and them flying on saucers had configured the reasoning of a lot of people, even those not born within the generation z to believe that saucers are always linked to aliens. As a result of this, whenever a flying object is seen in space, people are always quick to link it to an alien, even without having a real confirmation of what the object really is.

Over the years, there have been several rumours about the existence of aliens. A lot of people have come out at different times to give their own accounts of how they saw objects that they believed were aliens. When you look at these accounts, they happen to be similar in one way, which happens to be that an object was seen flying, and because of the belief that aliens were meant to fly on a saucer, these people believe that these objects were aliens.

Scientists have continuously conducted several research to see if they could come up with proof of the existence of aliens, but there has been no clear proof of the existence of aliens. During those times that people had complained of sighting aliens, even after running a check, no proof had really come out of it. But a lot of people still believe that as big as the world is, there's no way humans can be alone. There must be other creatures that are as intelligent as humans, or a bit less intelligent than humans, or even a bit more intelligent than humans that live out there but are trying as much as possible to hide their existence from humans.

Even after scientists have continuously come out to tell us that aliens don't really exist, will we blame people for believing in the existence of aliens? No! We won't blame them. When you think about this logically, the existence of aliens does make a lot of sense. The world is a big place with so many creatures existing in different parts of the world. How can humans possibly be the only most intelligent creatures in the world? Perhaps there might be some other intelligent creatures out there, but if this is true, don't you think humans have a lot to worry about? If there are really living beings out there that are as intelligent as humans and they have managed to keep themselves hidden from humans for thousands of years, don't you think they could be more intelligent than humans? No one knows; they could even attack the earth one day.

The belief in the existence of aliens that fly on a saucer must have been what led a local farmer, Shu Mansheng, in Ashu village on the outskirts of Wuhan, Hubei province in China, to invent his flying saucer. He could have invented a flying suitcase or, a flying car, or even a flying motorcycle, but he chose a saucer. The deception was believed to have cost him $3,135 to construct. To the surprise of many, Shu Mansheng wasn't a University engineer; he was a junior middle school graduate. His flying saucer measured around 18 feet in diameter and was powered by eight motorcycle engines.

CHAPTER 5: WEAPONS OF WAR YOU NEVER HEARD OF

EXPLOSIVE RATS

Have you ever had a rat in your home? Not a pet rat, but an uninvited rat that tries to share the space of your home with you. Well, if you've had one in your home, you'll know the true definition of frustration.

Nobody feels comfortable having an uninvited guest come and stay at their home. You might be cool about having them sometimes, but it would have been better if they had told you beforehand that they were coming so you'd prepare your mind and surroundings to have them around. Okay, you can at least deal with having an uninvited guest around for a couple of minutes or even a couple of hours, but what about when you believe they've overstayed their welcome, and you want them to go, but they aren't showing any sign that they want to leave? Some people will be bold enough to tell these guests that it's time to leave. These bold people believe that they wouldn't like to please others and displease themselves. For them, self-love entails loving themselves first, and that isn't a bad thing at all. But what if, after telling these guests that it's time to leave and, they tell you that they want to stay? And you insist that they must leave your home and even try to force them to leave. But as you try forcing them to leave, they run into the darkest part of your home and occupy there, refusing to leave your home. The more you try to chase them out of your home, the more they enlarge their territory within your home. They continue to enjoy your space and steal from your food without your permission. What would you do if you found yourself in this situation? Think about having a rat in your home and try to find out if there is any difference between having a rat in your home and the described situation. You'll get to find out that they're just the same.

Rats are very clever and intelligent mammals whose all their thinking is well-fashioned on how to take what isn't theirs and how to stay at places where they're not wanted. The most heartbreaking thing about having a rat in your home is that they would never be considerate to you. Imagine having a roommate that is never considerate to you, and you'll always want them to leave the house.

These rats will never agree to share your rent with you. If the rents are going higher and you're becoming bothered about how to pay them, rats will never care to share the rent with you, even though they occupy a lot of space in your home and move very freely within your home.

Have you ever seen an organism that will have its kids where they're clearly not wanted? Well, a rat happens to be one of these organisms. No uninvited guest will feel so comfortable having their kids that the owner of the house is fighting to kick them out. But the rat doesn't care at all. Even though they won't contribute to rent and would never pay for groceries, they still would have their kids within your space and would instruct them to go about your home the way they like. Now, you find yourself in a more difficult situation. You must have been struggling to kick a single rat out of your home, but now, you're like five more rats to kick out of your home. The nuisance continues, and your life continues to become more difficult and annoying because of your uninvited guest who had refused to leave and even brought babies to come to stay with them at your own expense.

While nobody really enjoyed having rats staying in their space, the British military found another use for rats during World War.

Imagine rats becoming very valuable and highly sought after. A lot of people would be thankful for having their uninvited guests refusing to stay with them. Will there ever be a world like that? Well, that was what happened during World War. Rats became very valuable since the British military needed them for something very special. There weren't too many ammunitions invented. Every party involved in the war were doing their best to come up with an innovation that would put them ahead of their rivals. There were very intelligent people then, and these people were brainstorming on what to create that would give them the upper hand over their opponents. There was something that was well known, and it was the fact that as one party was brainstorming on what to invent that would help them win their opponent, their opponent was also brainstorming on what they'd invent that would help them win. They were all very careful. They already knew that their opponents were thinking of ways to pull them down, ways that wouldn't ever come to their mind or ways they would never think of. Disguise was a very important factor because once the enemy found out about your plan, everything was ruined. This was why the British military had to think beyond what they believed their German opponents would be thinking, and they had to take their reasoning in the direction they believed their German opponents would never think of, resulting in the invention of explosive rats.

The British believed that once the Germans saw rats in their camp, there was no way their attention would be drawn to the fact that those rats were going to become the beginning of their pain. Rats were common in the camps then, so seeing a rat wouldn't be an issue, but there was something peculiar about these rats that the British military was using. These rats had to be dead for them to be easily used.

The explosive rats were made of dead rats. So, if the rats were still alive by the time they got them, they'd have to kill them. In fact, getting a living rat was preferable, and then getting them killed before using them. If one had to look for a dead rat, there were chances that the dead rat would have decayed by the time they would be found. Dead rats that had decayed were no fun to use. So, the rats would at least still be fresh for them to be fun to use. So, what the Special Operations Executive branch of the British military did was that they would bring these dead rats and fill them with small explosives.

Whoever they came up with this invention must have been very imaginative. When you think about it, you'll find yourself asking yourself questions like, what were they really thinking? These people were able to turn their nuisance into something useful to them. But is it easy to catch a rat? Like, how easy is it to catch a living rat? It must have taken a lot of work. Unless if they had at least trained those rats and kept them specially for the operation. A lot of people train rats these days and keep them as pets, but the species of rats that were used for making these explosives weren't the kinds of rats that one would like to train as pets; they were rats that people would like to kick out of their homes the moment they walk in.

Before the British military started making these explosive rats, they already had plans on how they were going to unleash them on their German enemies. Then, when you're trying to be innovative about a weapon of war, you'll have to also think of ways you would use it to get effective results. In fact, how to make use of these weapons and get effective results was of more priority than the weapon itself. This was because they had very limited resources. There were many soldiers who were dependent on these limited resources; they didn't want to waste them on things that would never yield positive results. There must have been other innovative ideas that other intelligent people must have come up with in the British military camp, but the

British military decided to adopt the explosive rat because it seemed more reasonable. The plan was to infest the German's coal supply with these explosive rats. The British military had expected that if these explosive rats were shovelled into a broiler at a military base, they would explode and result in a lot of casualties in the German military camp. It was a smart invention, but the German military were also smart in their own way, that they were able to discover the plans of the British military. Perhaps they must have had some casualties before they were able to come to knowledge of the plans of the British military. The discovery of this plan by the German military hindered the British military from achieving their objectives the way they had projected because the German military became very careful around dead rats.

THE OGBUNIGWE

Africa had always been known to source most of their military equipments from Western countries. But the first time situation led a region in Africa into producing their own war equipment, it resulted to something no ine had ever thought of.

History had always shown us that situations are mother of inventions. Most of the early inventions made by man were as a result of situations. Man found themselves in a certain situation which they weren't comfortable with. They decided to provide solution to that situation. At the bid of trying to provide solution to that situation, they were able to come up with an invention that they never imagined they could come up with.

The early humans used horses for transportation, but at one point, they found out that horses had limitations. Horses are animals. Animals get tired and at least need a lot of rest. Horses can fall sick and die even while on the route of transportation. Horses can't fly. Horses can't sail on a sea. All of these limitations made man to start thinking about what could replace a horse. They came up with bicycle, motorcycle, car, aeroplane, and others. Today, we've very modernized bicycle, motorcycle, cars, and aeroplanes. The ones we've now are so different from the ones that we had when they were first invented, but the point is that situations led to creating them.

Nigeria, the most populous country in Africa, at one point had a civil war which started from 6th July 1967 to 15th January 1970. The war divided the country into two parts with one part dominated by the Igbo while the other part dominated by the Yoruba and Hausa. The part dominated by the Igbo wanted a nation called Biafra after they believed their region had been marginalized for too long, but the Nigerian government refused. This led to a full scale war. The Nigerian military had a lot of weapons at their disposal while the Biafran military had next to nothing. The Biafran military needed to stay in the war for them to win. They had no weapons and they were blocked from acquiring weapons by the Nigerian government. This led them into making weapons by themselves. They went into quick research which resulted in the invention of the Ogbunigwe which happened to be the first rocket to be wholly designed, developed, mass-produced and launched in Africa.

The Ogbunigwe came in different types. The first type that was designed was the rocket propelled surface to surface missile which was initially designed as a surface to air missile, but was later improvised because of situations.

THE LARGEST GUN IN THE WORLD

Have you ever imagined about what the largest gun in the world would look like? Thinking about the existence of the largest gun in the world would look like will take you beyond what we've in our current days. There is no current gun in the world that is big enough to be called the largest gun in the world. Why? Because we already had one in the past.

The largest gun in the world was owned by no other but Adolf Hitler. We can't talk about war history without talking about Hitler because of the unrest he caused in the world as a result of his quest to conquer the world.

At one time, Hitler was eager to invade Frace. He wanted to deal a huge blow on France, such that never would have been heard of and would never be heard of. As a result of this, he started thinking about something no other soldier could think of, a large gun. When we talk about large gun, we mean a gun large enough to the point that it can't be carried by fifty people. Imagine what this gun looked like.

So, Hitler was so determined that with a large gun, he would easily pierce the concrete fortifications of the French Maginot Line, this was like the only major physical barrier standing between him and the rest of Western Europe. He didn't want anything stopping him from achieving his ambition, so he wanted to tear down the barrier and reign supreme over his opponents.

In 1941, German steelmaker and arms manufacturer, Fredrich Krupp A. G. Started constructing Hitler's Gustav gun. There were a lot of work to be put in place to get what would look impressive to Hitler. He already gave a description of what he wanted and Fredrich Krupp A. G. didn't want to fail him.

Hitler's opponents never imagined what was been constructed against them. It was what the war was all about, using weapon of surprise and disguise, weapons that will have superior might over whatever your opponents have, and this was what Hitler was going to do. He believed the largest gun in the world would show off his might and make his opponents fear him the more. But one thing about challenging an opponent is that once you're thinking extensively on how to win your opponent and make them stay down, your opponents are also thinking on how to win you and make you stay down. Even when your opponent is not expecting to win, they'll always look for how to last longer in the fight, cause a lot of damages to you, and maybe win you after a little moment of weakness from your end.

While Hitler was busy constructing his largest gun in the world, there were things he wasn't thinking, and this was something his opponents already had as an upper hand against his weapon of mass destruction. The gun was a four-story, 155-foot-long gun, weighing 1,350 tons, and shot 10,000-pound shells from its mammoth 98-foot barrel. It was really a large gun with powerful capacity, but it's size became its most weakness which Hitler never saw.

The gun was so big and heavy that it could only be transported through rail system. This made the gun to be an easy target to Hitler's opponents. When weapons are been moved over a long distance by rail, there were no guarantee that they wouldn't be ambushed. The fact that the gun was transported by rail made it easy target for Allied bombers. Hitler had no other option but to discontinue the project after just a year after he was faced with reality.

Don't forget to scan the QR Code to get all bonus content!